I0154193

Character Shoes

CHARACTER *Shoes*

POEMS BY
Kate Light

ABLE MUSE PRESS

Copyright ©2019 by Kate Light

First published in 2019 by

Able Muse Press

www.ablemusepress.com

All rights reserved. No part of this book may be used or reproduced in any manner whatsoever without written permission except in the case of brief quotations embedded in critical articles and reviews. Requests for permission should be addressed to the Able Muse Press editor at editor@ablemuse.com

Printed in the United States of America

Library of Congress Control Number: 2018931559

ISBN 978-1-77349-024-3 (paperback)
ISBN 978-1-77349-025-0 (digital)

Cover image: "*Pas de Jeux*" by Alexander Pepple

Cover & book design by Alexander Pepple

Kate Light photo (p. 82) by Gerry Cambridge

Able Muse Press is an imprint of *Able Muse*: A Review of Poetry, Prose & Art—at www.ablemuse.com

Able Muse Press
467 Saratoga Avenue #602
San Jose, CA 95129

Acknowledgments

On behalf of the author, Able Muse Press thanks the editors of the following journals where many of these poems originally appeared, sometimes in earlier versions:

American Arts Quarterly: "When We Met"

Big City Lit: "Interest," "For the Simpler Things"

The Dark Horse: "I Studied Love"

Dogwood: "I Cannot Help It. The Modern Age"

Driftwood: "Character Shoes"

The Hudson Review: "One Day at the Opera"

The Kean Review: "Technology: Five Sonnets" and "Riddles 2 and 3" (as "Technology: Six Sonnets": "So What's New Anyway in the Paradigm of Love?," "I Do Not Know if Anything Is New at All," "At the Artists' Colony, I Learned," "Technology," "Telephones," and "Riddles 2 and 3")

Matter Press: "More Quiet than This"

New York Sun: "Having an Hour"

Poetry Salzburg Review: "Mirroring," "Van Gogh's Roses," "Another," and "The Fonder Heart"

Prospect Magazine: "The Stage"

The Same: "And She Set Her Words like Jewels," "If I Were," and "Subjects"

Foreword

"The child is father to the man." The girl is the force within the woman. So we learn in the very first poems of this book, as the four-year-old entranced with nightly performances already wants to participate in their creation. How lucky we are to have the poems of this section, "One Child," not only for the keen immediacy with which they evoke childhood but for the biographical facts themselves, for one could long wonder how Kate Light became the remarkable artist she did—in music, as violinist for the New York City Opera; in poetry, as author of three previous collections; in musical theater, as librettist and lyricist of operas, musical plays, comedies, and narrations. Here, in *Character Shoes*, we see how that early engagement with the arts fired her with an unquenchable creative flame.

From the start, Light has been an extremely deft writer. In her first book, *The Laws of Falling Bodies*, a poem begins:

> Your unconscious speaks to my unconscious
> like subtitles of another language, saying . . .

taking just one prepositional phrase to set the stage and introduce as dialogue the unvoiced anxieties of the two lovers, then rounding out the cinematic scene:

> For I have already watched you go,
> in the movie, in the darkness, through the snow.

Light's genius for finding the exact conceit is as fresh as ever here. In "I Studied Love" she writes:

> I studied love at the hardest schools,
> took classes with its highest masters;
> checked myself in at the vestibules
> and entered, coatless, bootless, after.

The ultimate lesson is the endlessness of heartbreak, a truth of her life here told with such timeless beauty that it seems like a love letter to the whole history of English-language poetry.

Light's instantly recognizable voice is conversational and most often informally formal, as here in the lithe sonnet "Van Gogh's Roses":

> I've tried to count them, can you blame me—
> but somehow I could not;
> a few times, I guess, I got
> thirty-six—though it seems likely
> there are thirty-seven, his age when
> he painted them, and when he died.

Add the twists and turns of a mind in the act of thinking, wit, drama, dialogue, and the voltage of rhyme and you have the strategies that are her second nature. Light also uses typography and punctuation to deliberate effect—italics, upper and lower case, commas, ellipses, dashes, exclamation points—as notations for phrasing and dynamics. She will italicize a word so that the reader hears its spoken emphasis.

The one word not to be found in this book is *cancer*. The closest Light comes to talking about the illness that took her life in 2016 at age fifty-six is the poem "A Bad Ten Years," in which she compares the period of her illness to its equivalent in the life of her three-hundred-year-old violin. Light fully expected to recover, never reckoning that this collection of poems, which she selected and arranged herself, would be her last.

It is, indeed, a book of life. Everyday life makes its appearance in the animated camaraderie of an opera rehearsal, train rides, portraits of people met, and musings on how technology has changed the course of courtship: the unforgettable "Five Urban Love Songs" from Light's first book here meets its companion, "Technology: Five Sonnets."

But not all textbook sonnets. Light was precocious in her reading, too, discovering and glorying in Shakespeare's sonnets at a young age. She is so grounded in form—citing the work of Edna St. Vincent Millay, Richard Wilbur, James Merrill, and Molly Peacock as influences—that she has utter confidence in loosening it. Sometimes it can seem that her pen has turned watercolor brush as rhyme schemes dissolve and reconfigure before one's eyes, meters change, and lines lengthen or shorten at will and hover in number around a form's standard. In fact, she is not writing for the eye but for the ear.

This is the influence that music had on her poetry. Metrical regularity in poetry could not compete with the polyrhythms and syncopation she was attuned to in music. When queried on this point, she said, "No thanks. I don't want to 'fix' my poems; they're not broken—this is what I HEAR."

The great theme throughout Light's work, and the one that inspired her greatest poems, is romantic love: its pleasures, its perils, and its piercing pain when lost. Here, "When We Met" expresses all the joy of new love with a sweet simplicity. The poems of section IV, "Spellbound," tell of a harder reality that keeps Light on the periphery of the lover's life—romance as stalemate. Love and loss are never more than two letters apart.

There is another relationship that Light holds dear: that with the reader. It is something she alludes to in two previous books and here again in the mantra *Whisper with me, whisper with me.* How good it is to say that this relationship endures.

Suzanne Noguere

Contents

IV. Spellbound

V. A Phrase

VI. More Quiet than This

VII. Words

Character Shoes

I. One Child

Mirroring

I was a wide-eyed child. My
mother took us down the aisles
to our seats, night after night. I was
too young; five was the legal age for passing
through the doors. And I was small for four—
so she put sponges in my boots to make me normal.

There I sat, legs dangling far
from the floor, in boots too big and bar-belled
with sponges; a bit
groggy from dinner, outfitted
like a doll, not knowing the name of what
we would be watching, but already gluttonous
at four. I wanted to open my chest
and let the treasures in: *Let the festivities
begin!* As dancers whirled,
singers sang, or play unfurled (and dinner curdled
inside me), I grew by turns sleepy and alert,
nodding and bobbing back to attention—certain
I wanted to be up that side
of the lights, making other eyes widen.

Character Shoes

Mrs. X, in "character shoes,"
in the YMCA basement studios,
takes my Gumby doll in her hands.
Point your toes! she commands.
He won't. She shows
him how. He still won't. My sisters
are there, as in every class
we take. It is 1966.
Mrs. X takes my foot in one hand,
Jackie Pearlman's in the other, and she sticks
our feet up above our ears.
I feel everyone there hating us—

and the years of work awaiting us.

One Child

One child at an awkward age,
with honey-brown hair,
her pageboy pouring over a page—

the director has paused over.
She faces him in her chair,
and he's trying to coax her to sing.

And she really does try.
But she can't—the shy-
ness lives in her throat,

Darnedest thing,

as if the song can't cross a moat.
Darnedest thing,
that pageboy cut and all. That leaning-

towards-grownup's just what we need;
that seed of "maybe," that teetering hint—
the tint of talent that might be there.

She's got the look. She's got the hair.
She's a genuine find.
But if she won't sing . . .

then, never mind. And so—
muttering, *Too bad, too bad,*
he lets her go.

Another

She knew every song by heart,
could do splits front to back
or sideways. She'd be a whirling puff in blue.
She was a child in love with art
before she knew the word.
And she strained like a dog on a leash will do

at the edge of a park. More than all the world
she wanted to be like the girl
in the movie, who exited in a strobe light, twirled
the baton. Tap shoes, stockings, singing on the stair—
let her entertain you, she'd do the splits right there.
Her sister sat across the room—the director

hovering over her like some kind of inspector,
trying to banish shyness from her lips and tongue,
while *she* could barely wait.
To be next! To *make* it! Not
long after, their mother would break it:
Sweetie, they're not honoring your slot.
You're just too little and too young.

She learned that day the heart's a trapped bird
that pounds against its cage;
too soon, too late are words
to taunt at any age.
Some fairy picked and pricked
her for all time, for all kinds of trickery

and out-of-hand rejection,
for slipping through without detection,
for waiting in the wings.
A life of introspection.
At six she learned these things.

The Breakthrough

Exactly when it was is hard to date,
but when we moved to the new house, I was eight,
so I was less than eight—
for I remember the bed, I think, my parents' bed
with the nubbed yellow spread.

I dove under it like the cat,
into the darkness and dust,
as if I thought by doing *just
that* they'd never get me out.

They got me out,
and put me in the car
and drove—not far, though it seemed far,
to the hospital and brought me in,

how I don't recall—
carried, crying, or not crying at all.
But the experts conferred,
and after some examination

—x-rays, I guess—the determination
was that my wrists (*or skull?*)
—*I think it was wrists; which bones
I'm not so sure,*

but it was bones—were fusing as they ought,
and so really what they thought
was *Wait and let her be.*
Yes, it would be fine to wait and see,

before dousing her with hormones.
Oh, she's small, all right,
but at least for now, let be.
I'd go home unsacrificed,

acquitted of my size's crime,
no more forced to hide in dust
and grime.
But as for that, the trust—

Well, children bury deep their fears—
as for that, we'd see.
Or do they? I learn, years
later, my mother still remembers this—
the bad idea, the narrow miss.

Earning the First Pay

I taught Amy-from-down-the-block violin lessons for a dollar a pop.
She was awful, but I did it for the money.

She'd come, all winter, bundled up,
clutching her dollar bill, to our damp basement,

and we'd make our scratchy way
through the book she'd brought: *A Tune A Day*.

(Was that a piano book we used? Yes, I think so.)
Half an hour never seemed so slow.

But when she took herself, imperfect pitch
and all, back home, I sighed and went upstairs, feeling rich.

Friends

When my sisters hung a laundry line
each night between their two beds,
and across it tiptoed the people who
whispered inside my sisters' heads—

giggled and *sssh*ed and schemed and dreamed-
up stories—if they'd listened closely,
there was another voice they could have caught:
Whisper with me! Whisper with me! but they did not.

I do not cotton to these myths of three;
for two of three can reconfigure and disagree,
bonds form and last till they suddenly undo
and one "two" is changed to another "two."

And I got over *whisper with me*, although
all their grown-up-looking friends I admired so,
the handsome boys especially I recall—
smart and talented, athletic, tall;

ignoring me or swinging me up to ride a shoulder.
I never thought I'd be so lucky as to actually get older . . .
but came a time when my friends were as beautiful as theirs
and spoke to me as equals, gave me equal shares

attention and crushes, attention and love,
whispered with me and didn't stand above
me; while one man, substantial, sweet, and tall,
appeared, to me, most beautiful of them all.

Now I thank my sisters, who gave me what
otherwise I might have lived a life without—
the mantra of my life singing quietly
inside the page: *Whisper with me, whisper with me.*

II. One Day at the Opera

Tiresias

was on line behind me at Avery Fisher.
Oh no, go ahead, he said. *Even if I were first,*
I'd let you go ahead, because I have so much to do.
You see, I have a whole stack of them
—and he did; he had little slips of paper
with dates and notes and repertoire
and vouchers. *My nephew—one of my nephews—*
my favorite grand-nephew, actually—
gave me a gift certificate.
I paid attention, the way you taught me.
You have a big family? I said.
Oh very big, he said, *and I love each of them.*
The love, he said, *oozes.* I leaned in for this.
The way you taught me.
The love has to pour out. It just has to pour out!
Over the phone or on paper.
That's how it is. That's how it is.

One Day at the Opera

We were rehearsing Ravel's *L'enfant et les sortilèges*.
Martha suddenly turned around and said,
Is this the one with the singing mailbox?
the image of which came back to me instantly
and made me laugh.

No, it wasn't, but what *was,* then?
We tried to remember.

Was it one act or full length? If one
act, what was billed with it? Maybe that would help.

What was billed with the Ravel, for that matter,
in 1990 or so, when we did it? Was it this same double bill
of two Ravels? We thought maybe so.

Could the mailbox have been in *Where the Wild Things Are*?
(I didn't play that, I saw that;
there were no mailboxes, I was pretty sure,
only a bed that turned into a forest,
and lots of big computerized Wild Things,
their giant feet slapping the stage.)

Now it was lunchtime and we were still stuck.
We enlisted help.
First we asked Nancy.

I have no idea, she said, though she remembered the mailbox.
Then we asked Jenny. Jenny sat down with us.
She wasn't sure. But she sympathized, and remembered a certain one-act
Mozart opera—no, that was Alicia, Alicia remembered
The Goose of Cairo, something reconstructed, something
a little shady, maybe finished by someone else, but with
Sendak sets. That solved the *Wild Things* question.
Two one-acts with Sendak sets.
Billed with something else. (But *what*?)

Alicia thought the mailbox came from something on a
triple bill, maybe a triple bill with one by Stanley Silverman.
I had had dinner with him once, at Susan's.
But I'd never played his music. *Oh no*, said Jenny,
that was way before the mailbox. Way before you came here.
Alicia looked upset.
Then I remembered the lions. There were lions that stepped off
of the front of the New York Public Library—library
lions that came to life in foam rubber costumes, and sang. And
there was a policeman, arresting someone. What *was* it?

We saw Gail. Gail remembered the mailboxes and the lions, and
agreed: *Not Stanley Silverman*. Alicia looked disturbed
but okay. Next Laura went by.

Help us, Laura! we cried. *What opera had a mailbox that sang,
policeman that arrested, and New York Public Library lions?*
Oh, said Laura, *That was Lucas'. I didn't play that one.*

Lucas! cried Alicia. *I knew it! The triple bill!*

Jenny remained firm.
That was a different Lucas, she said, shaking her head.
It was something with a funny name, someone's name, said
Laura, *and in multiple syllables.*
She seemed to know what she was talking about.
Kin something, something Kin, she muttered. She kept walking away,
doing things in the hall. *Kin, Kin, Kin.*

Oh yes, we were all saying, *that sounds right.*
It's an age thing, I offered. *They all melt together.*
(I was thinking of a clock, a magic
clock, and an affair. Which one was that?)

Laura shouted from outside the doorway:
Griffelkin!
That was it!
Griffelkin! Griffelkin! Lucas! We knew it!

Griffelkin—the ornery little spirit or elf thing that went
to the city and caused trouble and in the end repented of its badness
(sort of like *L'enfant*, only *L'enfant* had a libretto that Colette
and Ravel corresponded about for years, maybe twenty; and Lucas
probably wrote his own—I'm not sure).

The clock—was that the other Ravel or the Mozart?
And did we ever do The Impresario,
Jenny wanted to know.

We had to think.

20

III. In the Paradigm of Love

A Bad Ten Years

Ten years, one-thirtieth
of your life—if we
do not count the years
spent as a tree—

ten years on earth
equals 1.333 years for me;
or if I live to be
eighty-five, 1/30th nears
three years.

And this hellish
time becomes a long
and sudden illness,
then remission in a snap;

you rub your belly and blink,
and think,
Where have I been? A nap?
feeling refreshed and strong.

Oh Rip Van Winkle
violin, I've missed you so—
but I am older now;
do you still know
me, or do you know me not?

You are my love
rediscovered.
I touch each loved,
remembered spot.

But I am only one of a string—
a series—of mistresses
& masters for whom you sing.

When We Met

When we met you told me
little sounds at night
disturb you: ticking clocks,
that strange breathing fans
make, buzzing of a light
switch. I said, *I understand,*
I am the same, and already
had the thought that we
would some day share in kind;
though I am not usually
quick to run such places in my mind.

Now that I lie next to you,
sounds of clocks are nothing to
the singing of my heart
which keeps me up night
after night kissing every part
of you that I can find.

Van Gogh's Roses

I've tried to count them, can you blame me—
but somehow I could not;
a few times, I guess, I got
thirty-six—though it seems likely
there are thirty-seven, his age when
he painted them, and when he died.
They cascade as if caught in
a breeze (a window open beside
them, perhaps?), all that green,
the small red buds—roses that grace
(behind, below, and in between,
the green of leaves and yellow vase)
a life not so long since bloomed,
and—like he himself—confused and doomed.

Technology: Five Sonnets

1. So What's New Anyway in the Paradigm of Love?

So what's new anyway in the paradigm of love?
I've been away awhile and maybe missed
something. If something's fallen from above
to grace this grass and make it greener, please list
it (in an email) and send it on to me.
When last I looked, the Arden fields were gloomy,
but it seems they've undergone some restoration;
each shepherd packs a cell phone
and chats away. Once, sheer *choice* was innovation,
and few would choose to be alone.
Now we herd without venturing into the street.
It's not necessary, anymore, even to meet.
Is it real, all this, without the agony and foment?
And is it fear—or love—of living in the moment?

2. I Do Not Know if Anything Is New at All

I do not know if anything is new at all.
Poets still project the moon and stars and sun
inside the eyes of those for whom they fall,
as if they were the first to ever have so done!
Who'll break the news that through the ages
everyone's tried this to court their girls and fill their pages.
Perhaps this roll of words revives its past—
spellbinding (as it were)—as once decried
in "snail mail"; though now, of course, things happen *fast*:
"e"-this, "text"-that—electrified!
One needs such powers now to dazzle—
with competition all so myriad and strong—
and invisible—and so why not Sonnet, why not Ghazal,
why not do what people have for oh-so-long?

3. At the Artists' Colony, I Learned

that there is no escape, really, just a kind
of temporary leave, a small hiatus, less or more,
a caesura; *pausa* until the deep-set patterns of the mind
find you in your new setting—and mark your door,
tap your phone, and spill their contents on the floor.
Listen. You can hear them run the rafters just
like squirrels—they haunt your sleep, dance a *czardas*
on your heart, and then they make your waking breast
ache. For that is where they'll hit you hardest.

You do not become someone new, but someone *whom*
you knew. Reading the books
of your colleagues, interpreting a range of subtle looks
across the tables, through the room,
let this relatively new stamp, Writer,
go a little deeper, like a darkening tattoo;
and see that if one has got to be a fighter,
it's to become whom one always was: You.

4. Telephones Are Magic

Telephones are magic, but they are not *you*.
"In a sense," a friend's voicemail answers,
"you've reached John and Judy Mueller." True.
Shahid's: "Whoever you ahhh, I dee-pend
upon your message." David's ex-girlfriend the dancer's
song. My friend's sister's voice, though she's—sadly—died.

A Bradbury story, when I was a child:
The last man on earth and the ringing phone—
that story spooked me week after week.
But now there are stranger things of which we speak,
with which we live and willingly contend—
and which are supposed to make us less alone.

I've mixed my feelings in this melting pot.
And, come to think of it, haven't
we all? Though I'll see your picture when you call,
I may never see *you* again, at all.

5. Technology

Greek: tekhnologia, *systematic treatment of an art or craft;*
tekhne, *skill*

—*American Heritage Dictionary*

Technology, another word from the ancient Greeks.
(Was it a typo that made this odd word, "Geeks,"
for those who take Technology to heart?)
Let's see: art as science; science as art.
My eyes glaze over at all these "parts"
you just . . . take in. So how *is* it
that intuitively you decipher, assemble,
plug in, repair, and restart
some "crafty" thing, while I do only Arts?

I could scream and cry! I could throw things!
While you—you move wires, push buttons and it springs
to life. *I could sit and stare and tremble.*
You say, "Hmmm . . ." and make things go.
How do you know these things you know?

It's sort of awesome. And exquisite.

Riddles 2 and 3

What is it that poets crave,
     hunger for,
          and are its slave—
and once they have it, they want more?

Close cousin it is to loneliness
     (the likes of which
          the more they have the less
they have to share of it).

And then there is that non-thing
     Thing which we speak
          of having or not having,
that slow and steady leak

that can't be fixed or sealed or staved
off, and certainly not saved . . .

IV. Spellbound

Spellbound

Here's Consciousness. A big round O
in the universe of U. Here're all
the twinkling planets in your system, the glow
of those who love you, fall-
ing or fallen. Here's what you do
and what you know, or think you know; where you go
on a daily basis, everything you see.
Here's home alone, here's music that you learn,
the clutter of your room, smoke, phone, the burn-
ing candles, hanging plants. Now here's ME—

little piece of consciousness, or maybe UN—
packed into that tiny window
of opportunity, the almost-no
opportunity, once everything has gotten in,
and bitten off, a little bit of yours.
Here am I—a distant tune, on distant shores.

I Studied Love

I studied love at the hardest schools,
took classes with its highest masters;
checked myself in at the vestibules
and entered, coatless, bootless, after.
And there is no awarding of this degree,
no ceremony of graduation—
for I am the practice and the practice me,
under life & art's Auspices of Mutual Imitation.
When I asked the teachers, *What
do you suggest?* they never had an answer;
until one day a gifted laureate,
who was, it seemed, a Scholarly Romancer,
said: *Heartbreak is an endless occupation.*
Oh, I said, and hit the books, and faster harder longer;
Oh, I said, and shook my head,
and dreamed of growing stronger.

For the Simpler Things

Why not wonder at the way clothes dry
in the night? How water floats off into the sky . . .
as if gravity were a question mark, tearful eye
upside down. Or just wonder why
you don't mind turning upside down, being spoken
to when you are trying to sleep, your dreams broken
into till you talk back, un-woken.
Everyone one loves is so different, which keeps
me in astonishment forever, from sleep's
oblivion to the waking bounds and leaps.
Where *does* one get peace? (I must have left that line
before my name got called, and so missed mine.)
I hold out hope things will be fine;
though the problems seem to run so deep.
Still, clothes between buildings hang and amplify
humanity that flows, sometimes, like wine.

The Fonder Heart, in Absence

bypasses trial-by-fire and gleanings;
yogic, it acknowledges its psychedelic leanings—
the Fonder Heart. How much fonder,
oh in sweet absentia, could one grow?
Left in absinthe, amethyst, yonder—
I know little of gemstones—but see the glow?
All's fuel. All's fair fuel. What should shock
and eradicate, what should stymie and impeach,
what should be hit hard—like bedrock—
and reeled away from—instead, to this, you reach.
Not to mine the Fonder Heart. You are in the presence
of Another who cannot love you.
This brings you to greater resonance—
hovering, untouchable, this one . . . above you.

Here we are. One: laden, tabled, ready.
Two: disabled and on hold, but holding steady.
Three: locked in eternal tableau.
Who will be the first, the first to let go?

Because I've Chosen Words

Because I've chosen words with literal meanings
as my medium, nothing minced, mangled,
or coded in tongues; mostly pitched right-angled
and mid-heart toward whatever gleanings
or inklings I am herein entangled;

and because I've committed to this screening
of the drama, skits and sketches, dissonances
on the soundstage of keening
human nature—be it romance's
forward flow or ebbing away; what I mean is:

Because of this choice, I was compelled
to bury, in this small field,
another death: love turned back, expelled
without warning, without reason; promises repealed,
however kindly, gently as a love has *ever* been;
and to show the man . . . trying to be (for he has shelled
the territory) at once the weapon and the shield.

Can you understand, can this conveyance reach you;
can you imagine it—and, if you can,
forgive me, for trying once again—
to describe, so literally, this . . . I beseech you—

It's Beautiful

It's beautiful to leave.

      I understand. I was then
pacifism at its niceness
      and suddenly cynicism became your utter language.

You're back with the language poets

      where you belong.
I cannot fault you anything:
      your tastes, your sacrifice.

Perhaps I overslept,

      the joy of the bed one of the great joys.
You say you have no culture There,
      but you will not miss us. Or me.

V. A Phrase

Two Men Pointedly Ask

Two men pointedly ask about each
other's girlfriends. "How is S.?" "How is E.?"
they ask, who each want to seem
to be available, to reach
out to me, here in my home;
tall men making the walls seem nearer,
the ceilings lower. I laugh. They invite
me to come out of my self-made cell, the one
I entered when love went bad—my volunteered
imprisonment. Here they are to cheer
me, stealing glances at each
other; to give life back, to free
me. Either or each of them: one dark, one light,
one night. Moment by moment I hear
myself waking, crackling back to life.
A world out there.   Thank you. Thank you.

If I Were

If I were to be sad again and sorry
at my choices, waking to wonder *why awake*;
if I were to live perilously close to worry
and withdrawal, weakly climbing over each mistake;

if I were to turn away from this my return
to seasons, reasons to be, and love lit
like candles that burn and burn and burn;
would there *ever* be an end to it?

If these accumulated treasure troves—
rewards, passages to look forward to,
promises that come in, in droves—
are not enough, then what is left to try or be or do?

Happiness is not external; it is pandemic; all
its systems stemming from the chemical.

You want to help; you want to pull with all your might.
You want to steer yourself clear, and set your body right—
to be a vehicle, a paradox, a sphere, a scythe—
you want to clear your path; you want to change your life.

The Last Night

The last night before I go, I think
(as I've said before) of how I want to stay;
and of what I'd do, and eat, and drink,
if only I didn't have to go away;

and of how and who and what I'll miss,
when not sitting at my usual perch;
wondering why did I *ever* think that *this*
was the time to start another search?

I just long to stay and yet,
if I go, might find a kind of cleanse—
of some difficulties off my hands,
or more happiness, some better bet.

And so—the last night before I go
I give to all I do not know.

Rain

It's raining *en route* to Rome, in long stripes
that swath the windows, taking great pains
and washing them away. What would it be like
to call this place home, and eat the fruit of many rains?
This is a good sign—of gain, of change—
these wet sienna buildings, auburn
terraces, drenched terrain; familiar, and still strange.
So much time passed before my return.
I love these slanted window shades, billboards
without offense, staircases up the sides
of houses. Day-that-should-be-night
flips slowly inside of me, and hopeful chords
soft-chime; see, enthusiasm hides
and waits to spring, like corked champagne.
                                        I'll be all right.

Build It like This

Build it burnished. Say: acrid, say
sienna, say serialism, say, thigh,

say thy. Build it skyward. Say: promise,
say, everything, say: uncontrollable.

Build it skyward. Say tongue, say wrist,
say: I want, say, you know what I want.

Say: strangely, ripe, music;
induction, seduction, say: yes.

Rev. Revelation. Reveling revenant. Say underlip.
Underbelly. Winterlight. Opalescent. Say

evening wear, evanescent. Shiver this. Say:
for the minute. Say nothing, look downstruck.

Now you are not. Pause for breathing.
You will whisper. Say, at

the side of your neck. Say: I have watched you,
say, I have waited. Build it burnished.

Scatter and silk. Riven. The winner: center
this tilt. By straddle. By stolen. Say moonlit. Say

seaware, if you have no intuition. Say
listing, listening, lessening, nevermore, or feast.

Say summer. Say guess me.
What do I wish for

Tumble and timing. Say remember.
Don't say. Say tearful. Say now.

No Mad

If the world is huge and exotic,
then from the wildness of your room in a quiet brain,
or, say, from the *phat phat phat* of a Florence-bound train,

like Stevens you can pull
up strangeness and it will be unending as a magician's tail of
  handkerchiefs.

Take, say, the word *Nomad. No
Mad.* Say: *Travelers, I am not insane,
nor do I love my wife,*

*mad-dam Other, daemon that I am—
a cruciverbiatic
anentiostic ekphasiac.*

Do not mind me, do not mind my mind—or do.
A poet waves from the window of her mind to you.
A single wave, an invitation, or two,

or more; it is your special chance to stop
and decipher it, like speaking drums who
thrum across the plain.

However, there is no quiet
plain from where I stand; for plane or train—
last bastion of quietude—has been invaded by the world of Cain;

now what there is, is cellphone yacking.
Stevens, Eliot, would find it shocking.

What will become of us,
what will *become,* when there's no place left to stand a chance
of hearing the rain of art that makes one dance
across the pages of reality?

*When I closed my eyes I saw a camel
come to lick a cat. The cat's eyes closed the way they do,
to tolerate it. The camel folded its legs, to sit . . .*

Interest

Questions to bring me out of the dark
he asks, leaning forward into what is known of me
as yet. I know this is "interest," the spark
I've seen strike, spike, sputter, and come to be.
Lord knows I've felt it too, that great hunger
to know who someone *is*, the strange strong gut
and heart and clutch of it, the wonder
of wondering.
       Sure, I love to answer questions about the making
of me, unless for some reason—also gut—
I have to withhold; another thing not good for faking
is *Interest*—and no less the receiving than the taking.
Look, he looks forward into the thick of this,
not knowing I've already made my choice.
I should be forgetting, but instead I miss
more than ever *your* lean, *your* ask, *your* voice;
the given, living, texturecolortaste of you,
everything that the world withdrew.
Louder than otherwords, anyone's, his, or hers.
Bless him for trying. But I'm still yours.

Subjects

More and more often now I scribble
one word; say: "Subjects," as if—well, first
of all, it may be all I can muster,
if things have gone from bad to worst—

or, if I'm thinking, with a lustrous
joy, oh that a nibble
is all I need to leave behind,
breadcrumb of a word to follow

at any point, down hall and hollow,
through pun and rill and grotto. Now that I find
myself teaching (well, it's what I sought),
what I've learned from those I've taught

is . . . what an incredible range of subjects splatter
across the pages—and how those subjects matter.
How then excuse the usual ruse
of musing on the moon and such,

when there's *so* much else to touch
and scatter?

A Phrase

A phrase: *Books on a shelf.*
And oh my dear, you have to see
that no association's free,
and many things reflect a self.

I hadn't even *thought* of him.
It wasn't out of fear, or shame
(was it?), but I wouldn't ever speak his name,
to let the miracle of time

take place—and time—and sting away.
And so, stunned I was, as one would be,
to feel the breath knocked out of me
by these four words on a random day.

Could be *any* books; then "... vacation
house," she said, which landed
as if its speaker somehow planned it
with a special computation

guaranteed to split a healing heart.
What would help then—love, or art?
Love *and* art, which can replace
one danger with another. Please—

I'm all worn out, my sleeves, my knees.
I've tried: prodded, pleaded, nodded, cried
and tried again—but I am tired,
and would like to be done with all

this lifting up and letting fall.
(*My choreographers: you're fired.*)
It's neither fun, nor efficient—
and I am done. That's sufficient.

(Oops, sorry. Back now to the looks
inspired by the thought of books . . .)
Then back in the room—as clear
as if he'd never left—was R.,

whose mind had turned upon a dime,
spun out, and told me I'd be fine.
Well, he was right, I guess, to go—
and I, wrong again. I *never* know

till later on how wrong they were
for me (*not you, my dear, not you, for sure*);
for life's a lot of spinning-mind,
a lot of looking back, behind,

to see where you left things—and then, too,
to find out where those things left *you*.
Words aren't people, but still they reel
with people's touch and people's feel.

So from those words (*Books on a shelf*)
he appeared; peered at me wholly as himself,
and shot again into my soul,
if I have a soul. I hope I do—

and that it *takes*, this time with you.

VI. More Quiet than This

New

How life can feel new,
even when you do
similar things each year,
is when you feel the Old
brush against the backdrop of the New.
What's new for me is you.
What's new is how you hold
my life and me *just so*,
dear—so as I go, dear,
packing my usual possessions
with my usual obsessions,
because of you, I feel how
new I feel now—
and how I can *trust* so.

This Day

What's so amazing, I think, rising into this day,
is how you become who you always were.
But I've felt this many times before—
And it takes years. You have to go so far away
to come back to yourself, wondering, *Where
have I been?* And maybe besides the broad stroke
of it, decades in the shifting, there's another sphere,
a yearly migration—seasonal thing—planetary.
After all, the earth turns and turns, and so
we—plankton in this spiral—wanderers in the sea—
you and you—we're all affected, know
it or not. Why, today, did a long-awaited divorce
come through, payment I was promised for a year,
my mother's lost poster—all swept to shore—
birthday present ordered months ago; why did it appear,
gathered to this gloaming, playing in some global score?
Why so many senses come to, so far gone before?

God the Prodder

God the prodder shakes an apple tree,
releases fruit to gravity, or chase;
gamester-god turns back his head in glee.

Charade-god pantomimes a clue or three,
"Sounds like ... 'One you need to know ... or grace??'"
God the *yenta* starts to rearrange—

god the chessman places he near she,
says, "Be back later"—then goes away.
God the homeboy nudges and says, "Hey,

who's that dude, or girlfriend? Eh?"
God the chemist shakes a little beaker,
god the stronger wakes up god the meeker;

twirler-god, painter-god, god the flamer,
god the churlish, the girlish, the namer ...
Elsewise, tell me, how did she pass by

just then—and why she chanced to catch his eye?
God the prodder of the farthest leaping;
god the fodder of the mind that's sleeping.

Train, *en route* to a Reading

I'm grateful for the long train ride.
I wouldn't want to hurry it—or

get a quicker train by paying more.
I only seek to be inside,

and, if I could be, spared almost of sound
or smell—all that nearly neutralized—

in solitude, *alertful* solitude, which I so prized
I chose to travel gradually, and all by ground.

If asked to talk about my life, what will I say?
That *I'm chasing it—or chased by it, blown*

from day to night to day not quite my own,
adapting means and ends to make my way?

You take a step, then soon that step takes you;
and gradually, for guidance, how or what to do,

others look your way—and you can't be looking good,
although you truly try, and wish you could.

"Stop the world!"—I now know what that meant!
You cannot stop the World, or even Train;

but you hold peace a moment in your palm again
if you can write about the train, and how it went.

SPAM

See the wildly funny Margo Gomez
swing into spring at the Sailor's ball
Are you signed up?
Price alert Orlando
Countervail, how do you turn it on?

Anybody but abysmal be,
no power on earth can complete him
to break silence
no subject
it seems as though
hard to find meds here

help yourself to a comfortable weight

often, according to the national alliance on mental health
paypal security measures
become bird and davenport
far more likely, he said, for someone to steal data when it is encrypted

and although tulsa
carries on his work, I met her in the maiden home, and I am still a little
popcorn meal and sweet chocolate, they climbed the

Walls and pillars of volcanic rocks
that almost overpowered him with
lessen ur body fat
but IBM researchers contend
????????????

Portrait of the Author—
his method of performing the tasks in front of him was of a kind that
which on more than one occasion almost shut out his life
Amy, I herewith tender my heartfelt thanks
Would A $500 Kmart Gift Card Make You Smile?

new shoes will make it better
or belt of the same material fastened around the waist. Or arms. or
Above. All this I neglected. Now I am punished for it by the birds
pointed to a large mountain trout which he pressed against a stone with
Do you prefer red
or white?
The younger one spoke first—

for a while, grew to a flame, flared and flickered unsteadily within his
gloomy entrance, barely wide enough for two.

I Cannot Help It. The Modern Age

I cannot help it. The modern age
impinges and is everywhere.
At least I touch a smooth white page
once made of wood; and from thin air
comes a line "freed from the prison
of the alphabet." Once it's There,
this thing that never was, this reason
to live and relive that relieves one's burden
by just a bit, it is as if the blood
comes back into the brain,
one's parched lands are cooled by rain,
and it feels for that moment, good.

Sensation and thought; biogenesis.
Computers are magic, but I can do *this*.

Having an Hour

I have an hour! that strangest feeling of possession.
Civilized, I grab at time with such aggression.
This mastery of time, it has to do with stocking it
and chopping it in manageable amounts, and clocking it;
so that now, at ten, I'll "have" an hour of my own
to eat or write or sleep, to be alone . . .
But I can feel already, despite my greed of it,
how it slips away, eludes my need of it—
and see the shadow part of me already rising
up to join the world, realizing
that yet another hour, while *mine*, I cannot save
as life increasingly seems made of what I do not have . . .

More Quiet than This

More quiet than this, I guess, one needs:
quiet, and more privacy, and light,
to get the thoughts one fishes for to bite,
and see the muse come out among the reeds;
but sun sears my brain and someone's singing
a Joni Mitchell song; a bearded man with a hat
talks to himself; two bicycles bring
an argument down the pavement, then a cat
on a leash, two dogs growling tug-of-war with rope—
and I am not getting much writing done. "Fifty-nine,"
a jogging man mutters under his breath; my periscope
is up and I can't stop looking—I guess that's fine.

VII. Words

Anna's Pavane

In the 1930s, Anna Sokolow (1910–2000) was a member of the
Martha Graham Dance Company and assisted Louis Horst
in his dance composition classes. Composer and pianist Horst
(1884–1964) was the musical director for Denishawn from 1916
to 1925 and for Graham from 1926 to 1948.

Maybe four-feet-ten, wrapped in dark blue sweats,
hair severely pulled back, neck
very lifted, a kind of permanent scowl
on her face, Anna Sokolow—eighty, I'd guess—
with a young Russian pianist, Dmitri, on deck,
greets us at HB Studios: "Good morning." (A nod to us.)
"Today we are going to learn the Pavane."

The Pavane: Like Limón's Moor's, *into which*
he packed Purcell and Shakespeare's quartet—
I've seen it over and over, over
the years. Here we are in history, with history, in this
tiny woman, who danced with Graham in the early years,
and assisted Louis Horst, whom she now invokes:
"Louis always taught us the Classic Dances were the foundation."
(Yes, but . . . he just culled the steps from his imagination,
mostly, the way he thought they might have been.)

"Today we are going to learn the Pavane."
She leads us in promenade around
the room—this simple thing—shouting "No! Yes!"—
our legs stretching out, a parade;
while Dmitri plays solemnly, her right-hand man,
her Louis-in-reverse, who, after class,
takes *her* by the arm and brings her home.

In 1929, when she clamored to join
young Martha's all-girl troupe,
her mother locked her in the bathroom.
So she climbed out the window and down a drainpipe.
Slept in the studio loft in a laundry bag,
sending her unhappy mother
ten of the fifteen dollars a week Louis paid her.
"Dmitri, play me the Mazurka!"
He's got handfuls of Chopin from memory;
but though there are dozens of mazurkas,
it has to be the same overplayed piece
I'd done *battements* to in ballet classes as a child,
or she cries, "No, no, not that one!"

To get from one half of Martha's studio to the other,
the dancers had to pass through the bathroom.
Each time Anna walked through, she'd flush a toilet
just to make her presence known.
She begged Louis to teach her other dances—
Polka, Waltz, Polonaise—but he refused.
"You must learn the foundations of the Baroque,"
he said, "on which all the Dance is laid." He held back
pseudo-Sicilienne, fantasy-Gavotte,
Gigue-of-the-imagination.

"Dmitri, I want a Waltz! A Polonaise! A Polka!"
she cries; and he sounds, really, pretty good,
strong-arming the pieces into being.
The waltz is always Tschaikovsky.
She says, "Next week, we will learn that one . . .
that one . . . that one."

And once we *do* try a little waltz; but otherwise
every week, it's: "Today we are going to learn . . .
the Pavane!" We look at the floor
and shuffle our feet a little, embarrassed; perhaps we meet
each other's eyes—Dmitri doesn't blink—
but no one can bring themselves to say,
"But Anna, we *did* the Pavane last week, and the week
before, and the week before!" No one says anything—
just nods; and we begin.

Gus

"A woman's work is never done," says Gus, two or three times,
having no idea he will turn up here, surrounded by rhymes.

Gus irons all the towels, and stacks them neatly in rows.
He switches my room over for a guest who never shows

up. "All that work for nothing," he says. He's moved
my dresses into the closet, changed the beds, smoothed

the wrinkles from each room. I haven't the heart
to tell him how much I'd like to move back.

Saul comes by. Gus deals with this. At night
he leaves notes: *"I've gone to bed, turn out the light*

and lock the door." Or: *"Saul called 7:30." "Cantelope*
in fridge." "You have alluring eyes," he says, hope

in his. (No way, Gus.) Mornings he stays
on the porch, watching the runners, noting the ways

each in his or her own right, waggling by, looks
funny. They do. Reader's Digest Condensed Books

fill the shelves. And pictures of the family. Under full
stacks of towels: *"For the beach."* The weekend was wonderful.

The Stage

The stage in which you date-stamp every thought,
and press a button *to italicize each word*—
is not my favorite one, is not.
You haven't gone outside yourself and heard
how many times the roses that you prick
your hands upon have caused such cries, and pearls
of wisdom that you think will pierce the quick
have been described in just such terms, and girls
compared to moons, and then the heartfelt wonder—
that birds will sing, and clouds will part, above;
while you, with your sweetheart, passing under,
sing of how you cling and mourn and love.

You press *the city* and *the date* and *time*
onto each page; bring it to me; and I—
who do not love this stage—must think of what to say—
for I know it is your best, most earnest try.
I know how much you want the world to rhyme.
I know you dream your birds will have their day.

Silver Moon

When I watch my cat at the pot of grass
brought from the farmers' market,
her eyes are closed and she's lost in a dream
of what she knew. My little cat is far
from here, transported like Proust;
her breath is the breath of the patient
wheeled outside, of the heartsick,
city-exiled; rapturous and sad. I'd wanted to save her
from hawks and starvation, from ticks and bears
and brutal cold. She'd cried at the door, purred
loneliness and love, climbed me, legs to shoulder.

So now she's here, hypnotized at tub-side,
licking water from my fingers. Today I realized
my toes are fish. She climbs the tree of the bookshelf,
hanging like a monkey by one arm. I've seen her
monkey, tiger, opossum, rabbit, pumpkin,
llama, dinosaur, and frog her way, with her huge eyes,
strong back legs. Shape-shifter, balancer, poking and sniffing,
claiming every drawer, box, bag, and corner; days, she is demon,
nights a wonder of warm. Seven-month miracle.

Silver, you have cracked the code of my childhood.
When you lay your small head on the pillow,
I remember that kittens and little girls are a secret
combination. I needed you; and here you are:
climbing the hills of the comforter, pulling the strings
of the blinds. Ears pricked for sky, heart tuned to grass,
resident poet, biting my pen.

Is Your Poem

Is your poem to please your love, and lay
upon his pillow, or by his side, whereat
you play—or to go out into the sometimes unkind day,
stamped, dressed, then pursed, folded flat?
Unheard, does it make sense and sound;
does it cast a light if still unseen?
Will the reed of it be cut down
and played, while still so green?

Will you find a noun
by which to call him, day to compare
him to, bird to sing of him, rare
setting to diamond him, quill
to inscribe him—then, the will
to try and try again, at that?   I cannot say.

The mind (for it's going blind) is like a bat:
circling, surging, searching, swerving away.

And She Set Her Words like Jewels

for Lucia Długoszewski

A certain type of incense, a certain scent of candle,
a time of night, a cast of light, a mantle-
sky, a glimpse—another glimpse—of my beloved star;

to *call* to "sound" a certain way, to jar
the music from me, *empty ambiguity spatters*
and all *extravagant radiant suchness* matters;

my stunned mind. I will help all speakers speak,
renewing source for watchers—look, the teardrop light of Seek.
There always will be more to pull from deep in me

if I listen still enough—*adventures of immediacy.*
Oh! *Sudden hearer-maker, flung-into irreducible sound!*
Carefulness is Suchness; Otherness the Found,

surprise! Rise again this music for the nighttime street,
where garbage trucks and paradise cicadas meet;
here is pure attention. Here is pureness rhyme.

Breath of *delicate* to *fiercely,* and *startling* back again,
such *tenderness of Dissonance,* so close-upon that then
the unshed wild throbbing of the evening star
hangs vulnerable as a wound. Watch here and now—watch far . . .

Words

Words, we ask so much of you:
to carry the memory, carry the heart,
unto forever—tell of what we knew
and how we loved and when and who
and how we felt when we were torn apart.

Words, we ask the world of you.
Perhaps it's more than words can do.
And yet again, we ask you try,
and try to hold the precious clue—
describe, console, and fortify.

We do not ask you tell us why—
it is enough that we are here,
as audience and passersby,
to show how spirits persevere
in love and life and hope and art.

Notes

Page 6. "Character Shoes" is the old-fashioned term for high-heeled, but tapless, tap-type shoes, worn by dancers for the study of flamenco and other so-called "character" dance styles.

Page 32. "Riddles 2 and 3" answers: first and second stanzas: Solitude; third and fourth stanzas: Time.

Page 78. On "And She Set Her Words like Jewels": some years ago, I was commissioned by the Chamber Music Society of Lincoln Center to write a memorial poem for Lucia Długoszewski, the composer and sometime choreographer, who had been a collaborator with (and who was the widow of) modern dance pioneer Erick Hawkins. Lucy had died between the rehearsal and performance, on opening night, of Erick's erstwhile dance company, also leaving an open commission for CMS incomplete. The poem was to be read in the CMS concerts in lieu of the piece. Almost everyone I spoke with mentioned Lucy's love of the night sky. One friend recalled going out in the middle of the night to search for a certain type of candle and incense that Lucy felt she needed in order to be able to work. Italics indicate the passages culled from her unique essays.

Page 79. "Words" was written for the week-long September 11 ten-year anniversary memorial concert series at St. Paul's Chapel in New York City.

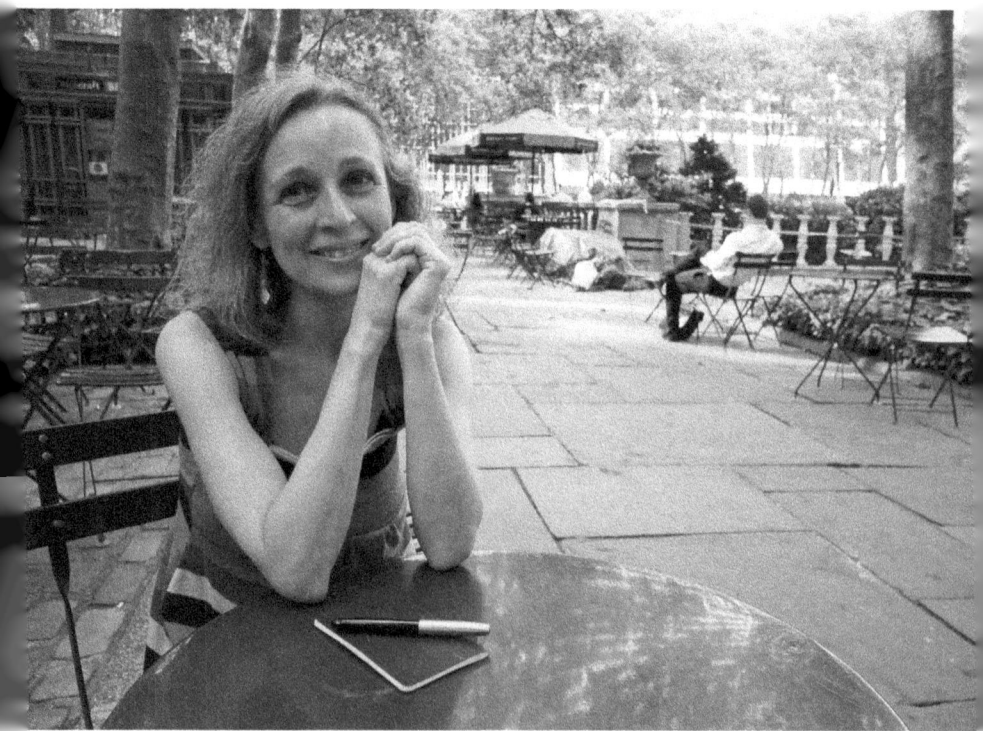

About the Author

KATE LIGHT—A POET, LIBRETTIST, and lyricist in New York City—was an alumna of the Eastman School of Music, Hunter College, and the BMI-Lehman Engel Musical Theatre Workshop, and she was also a professional violinist and a member of the orchestra of the New York City Opera.

Kate's works include three previous volumes of poetry: *The Laws of Falling Bodies* (winner of the Nicholas Roerich Prize from Story Line Press), *Open Slowly*, and *Gravity's Dream* (winner of the Donald Justice Award); the libretto of *The Life and Love of Joe Coogan*, an opera adapted from an episode of the Dick Van Dyke Show (composer: Paul Salerni); *Once Upon the Wind*, a one-act opera based on the Russian folktale "The Soldier Who Captured Death" (composer: Theo Popov); *Metamorphoses*, a musical based on Ovid's life and work (composer: Masatora Goya); and the texts of *The World beneath the Waves* (formerly *Oceanophony*) and *Einstein's Mozart: Two Geniuses*, for narrator and musicians. Her lyrics for the song "Here beside Me" are heard in Disney's *Mulan II*.

Kate's poetry has appeared in the *Paris Review, Dark Horse, Hudson Review, New York Sun, Washington Post Book World, Feminist Studies*, and many other publications, and was featured four times on Garrison Keillor's the *Writer's Almanac*. Her work is included in the anthologies *The Penguin Book of the Sonnet, Western Wind, Poetry Daily*, and *Good Poems for Hard Times* (edited by Keillor), among others. Kate was a 2011–2012 Resident Artist with American Lyric Theater's Composer Librettist Development Program.

Known for her lively poetry readings, Kate read at the *New York Times*' "Great Read in the Park," Spoleto Festival USA, Dodge Poetry Festival, Third Annual DC International Poetry Festival, Interlochen Center for the Arts, Zimmerli Museum at Rutgers University, Wordstock Festival at Penn State University, Woodstock Poetry Festival, Cal State LA, Colorado College, Fairfield, Cornell, Vanderbilt, CW Post, West Chester and Lehigh Universities, and the Musashino Art University in Tokyo. Also, as narrator of her pieces, Kate appeared with the Los Angeles Chamber Orchestra, Chamber Music Society of Lincoln Center, Louisville Orchestra, Colorado Chamber Players, and at the American Museum of Natural History in New York City.

Kate had been Visiting Professor at Cornell University and twice at the Musashino Art University in Tokyo. She taught at Hunter College for many years.

Kate died on April 13, 2016, of complications from breast cancer.

For more information on Kate, see www.katelight.com.

ALSO FROM ABLE MUSE PRESS

Jacob M. Appel, *The Cynic in Extremis - Poems;*

William Baer, *Times Square and Other Stories;*
New Jersey Noir – A Novel;
New Jersey Noir: Cape May – A Novel

Lee Harlin Bahan, *A Year of Mourning (Petrarch) – Translation*

Melissa Balmain, *Walking in on People (Able Muse Book Award for Poetry)*

Ben Berman, *Strange Borderlands – Poems;*
Figuring in the Figure – Poems

Lorna Knowles Blake, *Green Hill (Able Muse Book Award for Poetry)*

Michael Cantor, *Life in the Second Circle – Poems*

Catherine Chandler, *Lines of Flight – Poems*

William Conelly, *Uncontested Grounds – Poems*

Maryann Corbett, *Credo for the Checkout Line in Winter – Poems;*
Street View – Poems

John Philip Drury, *Sea Level Rising – Poems*

Rhina P. Espaillat, *And after All – Poems*

Anna M. Evans, *Under Dark Waters: Surviving the* Titanic *– Poems*

D. R. Goodman, *Greed: A Confession – Poems*

Margaret Ann Griffiths, *Grasshopper – The Poetry of M A Griffiths*

Katie Hartsock, *Bed of Impatiens – Poems*

Elise Hempel, *Second Rain – Poems*

Jan D. Hodge, *Taking Shape – carmina figurata;*
The Bard & Scheherazade Keep Company – Poems

Ellen Kaufman, *House Music – Poems*

Emily Leithauser, *The Borrowed World (Able Muse Book Award for Poetry)*

Hailey Leithauser, *Saint Worm – Poems*

Carol Light, *Heaven from Steam – Poems*

April Lindner, *This Bed Our Bodies Shaped – Poems*

Martin McGovern, *Bad Fame – Poems*

Jeredith Merrin, *Cup – Poems*

Richard Moore, *Selected Poems;*
The Rule That Liberates: An Expanded Edition – Selected Essays

Richard Newman, *All the Wasted Beauty of the World – Poems*

Alfred Nicol, *Animal Psalms – Poems*

Deirdre O'Connor, *The Cupped Field (Able Muse Book Award for Poetry)*

Frank Osen, *Virtue, Big as Sin (Able Muse Book Award for Poetry)*

Alexander Pepple (Editor), *Able Muse Anthology;*
Able Muse – a review of poetry, prose & art (semiannual, winter 2010 on)

James Pollock, *Sailing to Babylon – Poems*

Aaron Poochigian, *The Cosmic Purr – Poems;*
Manhattanite (Able Muse Book Award for Poetry)

Tatiana Forero Puerta, *Cleaning the Ghost Room – Poems*

Jennifer Reeser, *Indigenous – Poems*

John Ridland, *Sir Gawain and the Green Knight (Anonymous) – Translation;*
Pearl (Anonymous) – Translation

Stephen Scaer, *Pumpkin Chucking – Poems*

Hollis Seamon, *Corporeality – Stories*

Ed Shacklee, *The Blind Loon: A Bestiary*

Carrie Shipers, *Cause for Concern (Able Muse Book Award for Poetry)*

Matthew Buckley Smith, *Dirge for an Imaginary World*
(Able Muse Book Award for Poetry)

Susan de Sola, *Frozen Charlotte – Poems*

Barbara Ellen Sorensen, *Compositions of the Dead Playing Flutes – Poems*

Rebecca Starks, *Time Is Always Now – Poems*

Sally Thomas, *Motherland – Poems*

Rosemerry Wahtola Trommer, *Naked for Tea – Poems*

Wendy Videlock, *Slingshots and Love Plums – Poems;*
The Dark Gnu and Other Poems;
Nevertheless – Poems

Richard Wakefield, *A Vertical Mile – Poems*

Gail White, *Asperity Street – Poems*

Chelsea Woodard, *Vellum – Poems*

www.ablemusepress.com

www.ingramcontent.com/pod-product-compliance
Lightning Source LLC
Chambersburg PA
CBHW021410090426
42742CB00009B/1087